OXFORD BOOKWORMS LIBRARY
True Stories

The Love of a King

Stage 2 (700 headwords)

Series Editor: Jennifer Bassett
Founder Editor: Tricia Hedge
Activities Editors: Jennifer Bassett and Alison Baxter

PETER DAINTY

The Love of a King

OXFORD UNIVERSITY PRESS

Oxford University Press,
Great Clarendon Street, Oxford OX2 6DP

Oxford New York
Auckland Bangkok Buenos Aires Cape Town Chennai
Dar es Salaam Delhi Hong Kong Istanbul Karachi Kolkata
Kuala Lumpur Madrid Melbourne Mexico City Mumbai Nairobi
São Paulo Shanghai Singapore Taipei Tokyo Toronto

with an associated company in Berlin

OXFORD and OXFORD ENGLISH
are trade marks of Oxford University Press

ISBN 0 19 422978 5

© Oxford University Press 2000

Fourth impression 2002

First published in Oxford Bookworms 1989
This second edition published in the Oxford Bookworms Library 2000

The publishers would like to thank
the following for their permission to reproduce photographs:
BBC Hulton Picture Library, Camera Press, The Keystone Collection,
Popperfoto, Syndication International

Printed in Spain by Unigraf s.l.

CONTENTS

IN APRIL 1987

In April 1987, three hundred people came to a small room in Geneva, Switzerland. There were Presidents and Kings, film stars and millionaires. They came from the four corners of the world, east and west, north and south, and they spoke many languages.

But they all wanted one thing – to buy some jewellery. It was the jewellery that a man called Edward gave to a woman called Wallis.

One woman, Mrs Namiki from Japan, paid 105,000 dollars for a gold ring.

'Why did you pay all that money?' a friend asked. 'You can buy a gold ring in Tokyo for half that money.'

'Because Wallis and Edward were special to me,' Mrs Namiki replied. 'I never met them, but I'll keep that ring all my life.'

In the next few hours, in that small room in Geneva, the jewellery was sold for 50,000,000 dollars. But who was Wallis? And who was Edward? And why was their love story so special?

Let's begin at the beginning . . .

1

A Lonely Child

Prince Edward was born in 1894. His father, King George V, was a tall, cold man who did not like children. 'Why does Edward talk all the time?' he once said. 'He's a very noisy child!'

His mother, Queen Mary, agreed. 'It doesn't matter if Edward is happy or unhappy,' she said. 'A child must be silent and strong.'

The family lived in Buckingham Palace, which had 600 rooms. There were 8 kitchens, 19 bathrooms, 24 toilets, 11 dining rooms, 17 bedrooms and 21 sitting rooms.

Edward once told a story about the house:

Buckingham Palace was very big, and people sometimes got lost. One night my mother, my father and I were sitting in the dining room. We were waiting for our dinner. We waited and we waited, but the food did not come. After twenty minutes my father was very angry. He stood up and went to the kitchen. 'Where is the cook?' he shouted, 'and where is my food?'

'But, Sir,' the cook replied, 'your dinner left the kitchen fifteen minutes ago. Hasn't it arrived yet?'

'No, it hasn't,' my father shouted, 'and I'm hungry.'

The King left the kitchen and began to look for the food. Ten minutes later he saw a woman who was carrying three plates of meat and potatoes. 'What happened to you?' my father said. 'Why didn't you bring us our dinner?'

'I'm sorry, Sir,' the woman replied. 'There are a lot of dining rooms. I couldn't remember where to go. But if you return to the table, Sir, this time I can follow you to the right room.'

Edward did not go to school with other children. He stayed in Buckingham Palace where he had a special classroom just for him.

This is how Edward described his lessons:

My teacher, Mr Hansell, was a thin man. He never smiled and his nose was very red. We had lots of books but they were all very boring. They were full of words and they didn't have any pictures.

Sometimes I stopped reading and looked out of the

'Buckingham Palace was very big, and people sometimes got lost.'

window. Mr Hansell got very angry. He took a stick and hit me on the arm. 'Don't look out of the window, little boy,' he shouted. 'Look at the book.' He hit me many times and my arm was red.

Every Friday the teacher took me to my father's room. 'And what has my son learnt this week, Mr Hansell?' the King asked.

And the answer was always: 'Not very much I'm afraid, Sir. Edward doesn't like his lessons. He never listens to what I say.'

When Mr Hansell left the room, my father was angry with me. 'What's wrong with you, child?' he said. 'Are you stupid? Why can't you learn anything?'

'But the lessons are so boring, Sir,' I replied. 'And Mr Hansell hits me.'

'I don't understand you, Edward. You're a baby. You're so weak. You'll never be a good King. A King must be strong. Go to your room and stay there until the morning.'

'I spent many days alone in my room,' Edward wrote later. 'I never played with other children and I didn't have any friends. I lived in the most beautiful house in England but I was always lonely and sad. I saw my mother once a day at dinner time and I saw my father three or four times a week, but they never gave me any love. I was afraid of them and everything I did was wrong.'

2

The Prince of Wales

*I*n the spring of 1911 King George called Edward into his room and said:

'Next month I'll make you Prince of Wales and these are your clothes for the ceremony.'

The King opened a small cupboard and Edward started to cry. 'But father,' he said, 'I'm sixteen years old now. I can't wear soft shoes and a skirt. I'll look like a girl. Why can't I dress like other people?'

'Because you're different and special,' his father replied, 'and one day you'll be King.'

Edward cried for the next two days, but there was nothing he could do.

And so, on 10th June 1911, the family drove to Caernarvon Castle in North Wales and the ceremony began.

The King put a small gold crown on Edward's head. There was music and dancing and the crowd began to shout.

The new Prince of Wales closed his eyes. 'I feel terrible,' he said. 'Can we go home now?'

'Not yet,' the King replied. 'The people want to see you.'

Edward walked to the front of the castle and looked down at the crowd. He was shaking and his face was red.

'I can't wear soft shoes and a skirt. I'll look like a girl.'

'Smile, Edward,' the King said. 'You are happy!'

A few hours later the family were driving back to Windsor. 'Wasn't that a lovely day!' Queen Mary said.

Edward took off his shoes and looked out of the window. 'Never again,' he thought. 'Never again!'

3

The Royal Star

*A*fter a year at Oxford University, Edward went to fight in the First World War. He wrote:

I lived in a house with twenty-five other soldiers. At night we talked about our lives and our families. It was very interesting.

I could speak freely to different people – rich and poor, young and old. But I also saw the blood and noise of war.

One day in 1916 my driver took me to the town of Loos in Belgium. I got out of the car and walked to the top of the hill. Down below me there was heavy fighting and I felt very sad.

An hour later I returned to my car. I'll never forget what I saw. My driver was dead. While I was away, somebody shot him in the neck.

When the war finished in 1918, Edward returned to Buckingham Palace. One night he was talking to his father in the dining room.

'I don't understand why countries fight,' the Prince said. 'The war has finished, but nothing has changed. There are still millions of poor and hungry people. It's not right. Somebody must do something!'

'Well,' King George replied, 'you can't change the world if you sit by the fire. You must travel. Meet people. Talk to them. Listen to what they say. And then, when you are King, you can make the world a better place.'

And so, in 1920, Edward left England again. During the next five years he travelled 240,000 kilometres and visited 45 different countries.

He saw India, Argentina, Nigeria, Mexico, New Zealand, Germany, and Japan. When he came to Toronto, in Canada, there were 500,000 people in the streets to meet him. Everywhere thousands of people waited to see him – there were crowds of 190,000 in Cape Town, 300,000 in Paris, 500,000 in New York, and 750,000 in Melbourne.

'Edward is the first royal star,' one newspaper wrote, 'and he is now the most famous man in the world. In the old days princes were cold and bored. But Edward is different. He gets out of his car and walks down the street. Every two or three minutes he stops and speaks with the crowd. He laughs. He smiles. He shakes a thousand hands. He is a man of the people with a heart of gold.'

'I saw the blood and noise of war.'

4

The Meeting

*I*n the autumn of 1930 Edward went to stay with his friends Lord and Lady Furness. This is how he described that weekend in a book called *A King's Story*:

On Saturday the weather was cold and windy. It was raining heavily so we could not ride our horses. We decided to stay in the house and have an early lunch with some of Lady Furness' friends.

At one o'clock Wallis arrived with her husband. She was beautifully dressed and she smiled all the time. She spoke with Lord Furness for a few minutes, and then Lady Furness brought her over to see me.

'Sir, I would like you to meet one of my dearest and sweetest American friends, Mrs Wallis Simpson.'

'How do you do, Mrs Simpson,' I said. 'Please come and sit down.'

Lady Furness left us and we began to talk.

I could see that Wallis was not feeling very well. She had a bad cold and her eyes were red. 'I'm afraid that our English houses aren't very warm,' I said. 'We don't have American central heating here.'

There was a long silence. Mrs Simpson turned her face and looked out of the window. Then she said: 'You have disappointed me, Sir.'

'And why is that?' I asked.

'Because everybody asks me about American central

heating. I thought that the Prince of Wales would talk about something more interesting.'

I began to laugh.

'What's the matter, Sir?' Wallis asked. 'Have I said something wrong?'

'No,' I replied. 'I'm laughing because you didn't lie to me. You told me the truth.'

'But why is that funny? Doesn't everybody do that?'

'One day I'll be King of England,' I replied. 'And people are afraid of me. If I say that the sky is yellow, they say, "Yes, Sir, you are right". If I say that Wednesday is the first day of the week, they say, "Yes, Sir, you are right". And if I say that Scotland is bigger than Canada, they say, "Yes, Sir, you are right". But you told me that I was boring! You told me the truth. I like that!'

There was another silence and then Wallis began to laugh. 'Can I say one more thing, Sir?'

'Yes, Mrs Simpson, what is it?'

'It's your trousers, Sir.'

'My trousers?'

'Yes, Sir. They are black and your shoes are brown. These two colours don't look right together.'

I stood up and looked in the mirror. 'Yes, Mrs Simpson, you're right. I look very strange. The next time we meet, I will be better dressed.'

When lunch was ready, we walked through into the dining room. I sat at one end of the table and Wallis sat at the other end. I was watching her very carefully. I thought how beautiful her hands were. She began talking to Lady Furness and then, a few minutes later, she turned and smiled at me. I felt very happy.

After lunch, Wallis came over to say goodbye. 'My

Wallis Simpson
'She was very beautiful and her eyes were full of fire.'

husband and I have to leave now, Sir. We're going to another party in London.'

I wanted to speak to her but I could not find the right words. I don't know why. We shook hands and Wallis walked away.

I went into the next room and sat down near Lady Furness. 'Tell me about Mrs Simpson,' I said.

'What would you like to know?' she asked.

'Everything!' I said.

'Then perhaps, Sir, you would like to walk in the garden. We can talk more freely there.'

We stood up and left the house by the back door. We walked slowly through the trees, and Lady Furness told me about Wallis . . .

5

Wallis

*T*his is how Lady Furness described Mrs Simpson's early life to Edward:

Wallis was born in Baltimore. She never knew her father. He died when she was five months old. But her mother was a strong and loving woman, and Wallis was a happy child.

When she was twenty, she married a man called Winfield Spencer. For the first few years they were happy together. But one day Winfield lost some money in the street. He was very angry. When he came home, he took a bottle of whisky from a cupboard and began to drink.

Winfield Spencer   *Ernest Simpson*

That night he hit Wallis in the mouth. She screamed and
he hit her again. There was blood on her face and she was
shaking like a leaf. 'Please, Winfield,' she said. 'No more.'

But Winfield took her arm and pulled her up the stairs.
'You're my prisoner,' he shouted at her, 'and you're not
going to leave.' Then he pushed her into the bathroom and
locked the door.

The next morning Wallis went back to her family. 'I
can't stay with him,' she said. 'I want a divorce.'

'Poor Wallis,' Edward said. 'But what happened next,
Lady Furness?'

'Well,' said Lady Furness, 'a few months later she met
a fine man called Ernest Simpson. He's quiet, but
interesting. They got married and they now live in a
beautiful flat in the centre of London.'

'And are they happy?' asked Edward.

Lady Furness looked at the Prince and smiled. 'I don't know, Sir,' she said. 'I don't know.'

During the next two years the Prince saw Wallis once or twice a week. They had the same friends, and they often met at parties.

'Mrs Simpson knew a lot about life,' Edward once said. 'She loved books, food, people, and travel. She was very beautiful and her eyes were full of fire. She was friendly and easy to talk to and, after a while, I opened up my heart. We had no secrets. I told her everything. And that's how it all began.'

'His eyes were always sad,' Wallis said about Edward. 'And sometimes he looked like a child – so young, so quiet, so weak. He had no real friends. Perhaps people were a little afraid of him. But he was a warm and kind man. When he talked to me, I felt my heart jump. I wanted to be alone with him, but I knew that wasn't possible. Did the Prince love me in those early days? No, I don't think so. But each time we met, we just felt closer and closer.'

In June 1933 Edward gave a birthday party for Wallis, and during the next few months he visited the Simpsons' flat in London almost every day.

One evening, the Prince asked Wallis and Ernest to go skiing in Austria. 'I'm sorry, Sir,' Mr Simpson replied. 'I have to go to America on business. But perhaps Wallis and her aunt can come with you.'

'We went to Kitzbühl as friends,' Wallis wrote later, 'but when we came home, we were in love. And a few months later the Prince asked me to marry him. It was just like a dream!'

6

The King is Dead! Long Live the King!

*I*n January 1936 Edward went to Windsor for a few weeks. He was tired of town life and he wanted to work in his garden and ride his horses.

But then, one afternoon, there was a phone call from Queen Mary. 'Edward,' she said, 'you must come back immediately. Your father is very ill and I think he's going to die.'

When Edward arrived, he went straight to his father's room. He walked to the side of the bed and kissed his father's white face. The King opened his eyes and smiled. Then he took his son's hand and said: 'Be a good King, Edward. And be good to your mother.'

'Yes, father, I will.'

The King closed his eyes and did not speak again. Just after midnight he died.

Then Queen Mary took Edward's hand and kissed it. 'My child, you are now King,' she said softly. 'God be with you.'

His three brothers came to him, one by one, and they each kissed his hand. 'The King is dead. Long live the King,' they said.

At one o'clock Edward left the room to telephone Wallis. 'My father is dead,' he said.

'I'm so sorry, Sir.'

'I must stay here for a while,' Edward went on. 'But I'll phone you at the weekend. Nothing will change between you and me. I love you more than ever, and you will be my Queen.'

'Let's not talk about that now,' Wallis replied. 'You must go back to your family.'

'But you *are* my family, Wallis. You are everything to me. Goodnight. Sleep well.'

When Wallis put the phone down that night, she suddenly felt afraid. 'Edward is now King,' she thought, 'but what will happen to me?'

7

The Church

*I*n the spring of 1936, Mrs Simpson wrote a letter to her husband.

'Dear Ernest,' she wrote. 'You have been very kind to me. You are a good and strong man. But I must tell you that our marriage is finished. I am in love with the King and I want a divorce. Don't be angry. There is nothing you can do. I'll never forget you, but I have to be free.'

Ernest replied immediately: 'Your letter arrived this morning. I will do what you ask, but I'll never stop loving you. And if you need me, I'll always be here.'

That night the King and Wallis met at a small restaurant in Piccadilly. Edward read Ernest's letter again and again. 'That's wonderful news,' he said. 'Nothing can stop us now!'

The next day, when Edward came down to breakfast, Gordon Lang, the Archbishop of Canterbury, was waiting for him.

'Good morning, Gordon,' the King said. 'How nice to see you again. And what can I do for you?'

For a minute the Archbishop said nothing. Then he opened a small black bag and took out three newspapers. 'I have come to see you about Mrs Wallis Simpson,' he began. 'The newspapers say that you want to marry her. Are these stories true, Sir?'

'Yes, Gordon, Wallis is going to be my wife.'

'But that's not possible,' the Archbishop replied. 'You know what the Church thinks about marriage and divorce. Divorce is wrong in the eyes of God!'

Edward smiled and then said: 'Can I ask you some questions about God, Mr Lang?'

'Yes, of course, Sir.'

'Is God happy when two people fall in love?'

'Yes, Sir, but . . .'

'The Church is very strong, and we will not have this woman as our Queen.' Archbishop Lang

'And is God happy when two people fall in love and get married?'

'Yes, Sir, but . . .'

'And is God happy when two people fall in love, get married, and live happily together?'

'Yes, Sir, but . . .'

'Then, Archbishop, Wallis and I will make God very happy. We are in love, we'll get married, and we'll live together happily!'

'But you don't understand, Sir,' Mr Lang replied. 'The Church says that divorce is wrong. Mrs Simpson cannot leave Mr Simpson and then marry you. You must forget about her and find another woman. Please, Sir, I must ask you to think again.'

'That is not possible,' Edward said softly. 'When Wallis is free, I shall marry her.'

There was a long silence. The Archbishop looked down at the floor and shook his head. 'You're making a big mistake, Sir,' he said. 'The Church is very strong, and we will not have this woman as our Queen!'

Suddenly Edward stood up, his face red and angry. 'Thank you for coming,' he said. 'But I have nothing more to say. And I want to be alone.'

The Archbishop stood up to go, but then turned and touched the King's arm. 'Please, Sir, think again. The Church will be against you.'

'I don't care,' Edward replied. 'I have God on my side, and that is all I need. Goodbye, Mr Lang.'

8

The Storm

*I*n July and August Wallis and the King sailed the Mediterranean. They met Prime Minister Metaxas in Greece, Kemal Ataturk in Turkey, and King Boris in Bulgaria. But that summer is famous for Edward's clothes. On the journey from Athens to Istanbul, the King took off his shirt to get brown in the sun. It was hot, and ten minutes later he was asleep. So he did not see the young photographer who was now taking pictures of the King . . .

When Edward returned from the Mediterranean, there was a letter waiting for him.

It was from Mr Albert Thompson of Birmingham, who wrote: 'I saw a picture of you in the newspaper this morning and I felt very angry. I have never seen a King dressed as badly as you were! No shirt! And no tie, no socks, no hat . . . and in short trousers! How could you, Sir?'

Edward showed this letter to Stanley Baldwin, the Prime Minister. 'What do you think of this?' the King asked.

'Mr Thompson is right, Sir,' the Prime Minister replied. 'You want to be modern, but the people don't like it.'

'I have never seen a King dressed as badly as you were!'

Edward put the letter on the fire. 'And do you think that divorce is "modern", Mr Baldwin?'

The Prime Minister sat down. 'Yes, Sir,' he began, 'I've read about this Mrs Simpson. She has two husbands still alive. And you must understand what that means, Sir. She cannot marry a King.'

'But I cannot live without her,' Edward said.

'Then, Sir,' the Prime Minister replied, 'I can see there's a storm coming. I have talked to your family and to Archbishop Lang, and we will not have this woman as our Queen.'

That night the Prime Minister and the King spoke for many hours. There were hundreds of questions, but only one answer. And so, in the early hours of the next morning, Edward said:

'You tell me that Wallis cannot marry a King. So there is only one thing that I can do. I will give the crown to my brother, and leave England. I must follow my heart. You tell me that it's a crime to fall in love. You tell me that it's wrong to be happy. How strange this country is!'

An hour later Edward telephoned Wallis. 'The Prime Minister says that a storm is coming,' Edward said. 'So I want you to go away.'

Wallis packed her bags and left for France. Then Edward went to see his mother.

It was a sad, strange, and angry meeting. 'Do you know what you are doing?' the Queen asked. 'Look out of that window. Outside this palace there are 400,000,000 people who call you King. They need you. And you will leave all this for Mrs Simpson?'

'Yes, mother, I will. I'm in love.'

'Love?' Queen Mary shouted. 'You're a King! You must love your country first!'

'But I'm also a man,' Edward said softly, 'and there's nothing that I can do.'

That afternoon the King telephoned Winston Churchill, one of his closest friends.

'I have some sad news,' Edward began. 'Last night Mr Baldwin came to see me. I have decided to go away next week.'

'Do you mean on holiday, Sir?'

'No, Winston, I'm leaving England. I'm never coming back. George will be King.'

'But that's not right, Sir. You're a free man. You must stand and fight.'

'No,' the King said. 'I have seen war and it's a terrible thing. I don't want to fight again.'

'But the people love you. And they want Wallis to be Queen.'

'Perhaps they do,' Edward replied. 'But she cannot be Queen. My enemies are stronger than I am. I am just a sailor. And when the winds change, the sea moves and it takes my boat away.'

9

The Woman I Love

A few days later Mr Churchill came to see Edward at Buckingham Palace. At first the King was quiet. Then he said: 'This is my last night in England, Winston. I love this country. I wanted to be a modern, kind King. I wanted to change the world, but *they* stopped me. And now I have to leave.'

It was ten o'clock. Edward stood up and walked over to the window. In the dark streets below there were hundreds of people. They were singing and calling his

'But the people love you,' Winston Churchill said. 'And they want Wallis to be Queen.'

name: 'Edward, Edward, we love Edward!' they shouted. 'Long live the King! Long live love!'

Suddenly the King turned to Mr Churchill. 'Why is this happening to me, Winston?' he cried. 'What have I done wrong?'

He sat down and put his head in his hands. There was a silence in the room, but through the open window came the shouting from the street. 'Long live Edward! Long live love! Long live Edward! Long live love!'

Mr Churchill came over and put his hand on the King's arm. Edward looked up. 'Thank you, Winston,' he said. 'You were a good friend to me.'

'Thank you, Sir. And you were a good King.'

At ten o'clock the next morning the telephone rang in Edward's bedroom.

'They're ready for you now, Sir,' a voice said.

The King walked slowly down the stairs. In front of him there was an open door. The family were waiting for him. His mother sat near the window, dressed in black. His brothers stood beside her. 'How close they are!' the King thought.

On a small table in the centre of the room there was a piece of paper. Edward sat down and read these words:

I, Edward the Eighth, King of Great Britain, King of India, King of Australia, King of New Zealand, King of Canada, King of Kenya, King of Nigeria, King of Burma, King of Malaya, King of Singapore, and King of thirty-two other countries, have today given the crown to my brother George.

God be with him and all his people.

10th December 1936.

Edward took a pen and wrote his name at the bottom of the page. Then he stood up and kissed his brother's hand.

'I never wanted this to happen,' George said. 'This is the worst day of my life.'

Edward walked over to his mother. 'Before I kiss you,' she said, 'there are some things that I want to say. I have never understood you, child. This morning you

*'I love you. I am your mother and nothing can change that. But
if you marry that woman, you will break my heart.'*

were a King. But tonight, you'll run from England like a
thief. Alone. Angry. Afraid. You think that you're free.
But you're not. You cannot be free.

'Everyone needs their family. Everyone needs their
home. And tonight you have lost both those things.

'I love you. I am your mother and nothing can change
that. But if you marry that woman, you will break my
heart. Go now. It is all very sad.'

Edward kissed Queen Mary's hand. Then he turned
and walked away.

The next day Edward returned to Windsor Castle. He
went into a small, cold room at the top of the building.

'Earlier today I gave the crown to my brother George. He is now your King.'

From there, he spoke on BBC radio to Britain and the world.

This is what he said:

Tonight, for the first time, I can say a few words to you. Earlier today I gave the crown to my brother George. He is now your King. I will soon leave this country and travel to France. My heart is with Wallis and I cannot live without the woman I love.

I don't know what will happen to me. Perhaps I will never see England again. But think of me tonight when I sail across the sea.

God be with you. Long live King George!

Edward left Windsor Castle and got into a large black

car. It was now midnight and it was just beginning to rain.

'Take me away as quickly as you can,' he said. The car moved off into the darkness and the rain.

'What a night!' said the driver. 'I think the sky is crying, Sir.'

At 1.30 a.m. they arrived at Portsmouth. Edward got out of the car and a voice said: 'The King is here!'

Edward stopped and looked out across the open sea. There was a thin, cold smile on his face. 'King?' he said. 'No, I am not the King. I am just a man in love.'

Then he turned and walked onto the ship and into the night.

10

The Wedding

The next morning Edward telephoned Wallis from Boulogne.

'Did you listen to me on the radio?' he asked.

'Yes, of course,' she said.

'And how did you feel?'

'I was sitting in my room alone,' Wallis said. 'And when I listened to your words, I felt so sad. I put my hands over my eyes and I just cried. I couldn't stop myself. You have left everything for me. But I love you

Edward married Wallis Simpson on 3rd June 1937.

so much, Edward, and with me, you'll be the happiest man in the world.'

'I am that already,' he replied. 'You are all that matters in my life.'

Edward married Wallis Simpson six months later, on 3rd June 1937. None of the Royal Family came to the wedding. Edward was forty-three. Wallis was forty-one. And they now took a new name – the Duke and Duchess of Windsor.

A few weeks later Edward wrote to his brother King George. 'I was surprised that you didn't come to the wedding,' he wrote. 'But Wallis is now my wife and nothing can change that. As you know, we have a house in Paris. But France is not my home, and I want to live again at Windsor with Wallis by my side.'

'I'm sorry, Edward,' King George wrote back. 'But you know how I feel about that woman. I do not like her. I will never like her. You can live here, but Wallis cannot.'

'My brother', Edward said later, 'pushed me away like a dog. I will never forget what he did. And after that I decided that I didn't want my family. They didn't want Wallis, and so I didn't want them.'

11

Paris

*F*or the next thirty years the Duke and Duchess lived in Paris. They gave parties and travelled round the world, but they never went back to Buckingham Palace.

When King George died in 1952 and Queen Mary died in 1961, Edward returned to Windsor for a few days. But Wallis stayed in France. 'It's your family,' she said. 'Not mine.'

But then, in 1966, the Duke and Duchess met Queen Elizabeth (the daughter of King George) at a small party in London. After thirty long years it was time to forget the past. Elizabeth kissed the Duchess and touched her arm. Then she turned to the Duke and said: 'Wallis is so beautiful, uncle. I think you're a lucky man.'

'That day Elizabeth was very kind to us,' Edward wrote later. 'But why couldn't my mother or my brother say those words to me?'

On BBC television in 1969 the Duke and Duchess spoke about their life together.

'Do you argue?' someone asked them.

'No, not really,' the Duchess replied. 'But there's one thing about my husband that I really don't like. He is always late. It doesn't matter if he's meeting a queen, a

For the next thirty years the Duke and Duchess lived in Paris.

president, or a film star. He can never arrive on time. I don't know why. I have tried to change him, but it's just not possible.'

The Duke smiled and touched her hand. 'I know that I'm often late,' he said. 'But on our wedding day, I arrived at the church twenty minutes before you. I was early and *you* were late.'

'Yes, that's true,' the Duchess said. And they both laughed.

'You could see real love in their eyes,' one newspaper wrote. 'They were on television, but they forgot about the cameras and the millions of people who were watching. They were just two people in love.'

'You could see real love in their eyes.'

The Duchess was famous for her jewellery. 'After my husband,' she once said, 'I love jewellery more than anything else in the world.' And after thirty-five years with the Duke she had hundreds of pieces, which came from all over the world.

'I have never met a more beautiful woman than

Wallis,' Edward wrote, 'and I love giving her presents. She has given me so much happiness. I buy her jewels to say "thank you".'

In May 1972 the Duke became ill. When the doctor arrived, he listened to Edward's heart and then said: 'How many cigarettes do you have a day, Sir?'

'About forty or fifty,' the Duke replied. 'But please don't ask me to stop. I've smoked for sixty years and I cannot change now.'

That night Edward called Wallis into the room. 'I feel very tired,' he said. 'And I'm afraid. I love you. I have been very happy with you, and you have been a wonderful wife. When I die, I want you to take my body back to Windsor. Will you do that for me?'

'Yes, of course,' she said. And they both began to cry.

The Duke of Windsor died one hour later with Wallis by his side.

Three days later, a blue aeroplane arrived in Paris. Wallis went back to England with the Duke's body and, for the first time in her life, she entered Buckingham Palace.

A week later the Duchess returned to France, and for the next fourteen years she lived alone in Paris. The big house was dark. The doors were locked and she did not go out.

In the afternoons she sat in the dining room with Edward's love letters. 'They were so beautiful,' she said.

*The Duchess with Queen Elizabeth II at Buckingham Palace
after Edward's death.*

'I read them again and again.'

But then, in 1986, Wallis became ill. She went to a
small hospital near the house, and a few days later she
died. 'Without Edward,' she once wrote, 'my life was
empty.'

She was buried in England next to her husband at
Windsor. 'It's a strange thing,' one newspaper wrote.
'When they were alive, the Duke and Duchess could
never live in Britain. It was only in death that they could
be there together.'

12

Long Live Love!

*I*n 1970, two years before his death, Edward said:

There are some people who think that I was wrong to give away my crown. But they don't understand true love.

When I was young, I lived in Buckingham Palace. I could have anything that I wanted. But I wasn't happy because my heart was empty.

Then I met Wallis and everything changed. For half of my life I have lived here with the most beautiful woman in the world. And she is everything to me.

When I sit in my garden with the Duchess by my side, I sometimes think about my early life. I remember the days alone in my bedroom. I remember the teacher who hit me with a stick. I remember the war and my travels around the world. And then I remember the crowds of people below my window, who shouted: 'Long live love!'

On my last night in London I spoke with Winston Churchill. In the middle of our conversation he said: 'I think, Sir, that the best things in life are free.' I have never forgotten those words. And now, many years later, I understand what they mean. You cannot buy happiness. And you cannot buy love.

To be happy deep inside your heart is the most wonderful thing in the world. I have been a lucky man. And so I say:

'Thank God for Wallis, and LONG LIVE LOVE!'

'She is everything to me.'

THE DUKE AND DUCHESS OF WINDSOR

1894   Edward is born in Richmond, England.

1896   Wallis is born in Baltimore, USA.

1911   Edward becomes Prince of Wales.

1912   Edward enters Oxford University.

1914   The First World War begins. Edward sees fighting on the front line in Belgium.

1916   Wallis marries Winfield Spencer.

1920   Edward begins a five-year journey round the world. He visits 45 countries and travels 240,000 kilometres.

1927   Wallis divorces Winfield Spencer.

1928   Wallis marries Ernest Simpson.

1930   Edward meets Wallis at a weekend house party.

1936   King George V dies in January, and Edward is now King. Ernest Simpson agrees to divorce Wallis. Edward tells his mother that he wants to marry Wallis. In December Edward gives the crown to his brother and leaves England.

1937   Edward and Wallis marry in France. They take the names Duke and Duchess of Windsor. None of the Royal Family comes to the wedding. For the next thirty years the Duke and Duchess live outside England.

1966   Queen Elizabeth II meets the Duke and Duchess at a small party in London. 'It's time to forget the past,' she says.

1972   Edward dies in Paris. His body is buried in England at Windsor Castle.

1986   Wallis dies in Paris and is buried next to Edward at Windsor.

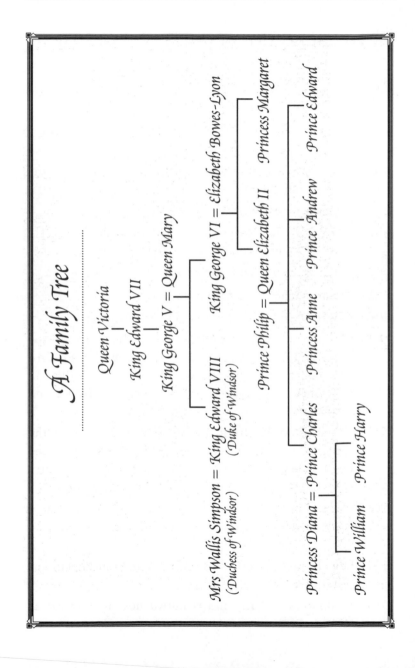

A Family Tree

Queen Victoria
|
King Edward VII
|
King George V = Queen Mary

Mrs Wallis Simpson = King Edward VIII   King George VI = Elizabeth Bowes-Lyon   Princess Margaret
(Duchess of Windsor)

Prince Philip = Queen Elizabeth II

Princess Diana = Prince Charles   Princess Anne   Prince Andrew   Prince Edward

Prince William   Prince Harry

Queen Victoria and three future Kings:
George V (left), Edward VII (right), and Edward VIII (in sailor suit)

GLOSSARY

Archbishop (of Canterbury) the most important man in the
Church of England

argue to say that something is wrong or not true; not to agree
with someone

aunt the sister of your father or mother, or the wife of your uncle

become (past tense **became**) to change and begin to be something

bury (past tense **buried**) to put a dead person in the ground

central heating a system to make a house warm

ceremony a special programme at an important happening (e.g.
a wedding)

crown *(n)* a special 'hat' (usually made of gold, etc.) that a king
or queen wears at important times

dining room a room where people eat

disappoint to make someone sad because the things they wanted
do not happen

divorce *(v)* to finish a marriage by law

dream *(n)* something unreal; a picture in your head when you are
asleep

fall in love to begin to love somebody very much

God the 'person' who made the world and controls all things

heart the place in the body where people feel love

jewellery rings, necklaces, etc. with valuable stones in them (e.g.
diamonds)

kiss *(v)* to touch someone with your mouth to show love

kitchen a room where people cook food

lie *(v)* to say something that you know is not true

mirror a piece of special glass where you can see yourself

prime minister the most important person in the government of
a country

return *(v)* to go or come back

royal of a king or queen

sad unhappy

sir a polite word for a man when you speak to him

truth something that is true

uncle the brother of your mother or father, or the husband of your aunt

war fighting between two or more countries

weak not strong

wedding the ceremony when people get married

ACTIVITIES

Before Reading

1 **Read the back cover, and the story introduction on the first page. What do you know now about this story? Tick one box for each sentence.**

		YES	NO
1	Edward VIII was King of 42 countries.	☐	☐
2	Everyone wanted Edward to marry the woman he loved.	☐	☐
3	She was the Queen of another country.	☐	☐
4	She was already married to another man.	☐	☐
5	*The Love of a King* is a true story.	☐	☐

2 **How do you think life is different for a king? Do you agree (A) or disagree (D) with these sentences?**

1 A king can choose his own wife.
2 A king has an easy life because he is rich.
3 A king can say what he wants and do what he wants.
4 A king is always followed by photographers.

3 **What will happen in this story? Choose one of these ideas.**

1 Edward marries the woman, and is still the King.
2 Edward marries the woman, and leaves the country.
3 Edward doesn't marry, and is the King for many years.

ACTIVITIES

While Reading

Read *In April 1987* on page 1. Can you guess the answers to these questions?

1 Why were Edward and Wallis so famous?
2 Why did Edward give Wallis so much jewellery?

Read Chapters 1 and 2. Now complete this passage with the right words (one word for each gap).

Edward was not a _____ child. He lived in a big, beautiful _____, but he never _____ with other children, and he had no _____. He didn't go to _____, but had _____ with a teacher, who sometimes hit him with a _____.

When Edward was _____, he became _____ of Wales. He had to wear special clothes and a gold _____ on his head.

Read Chapters 3 and 4. Are these sentences true (T) or false (F)? Change the false sentences into true ones.

1 In the First World War Edward only met rich people.
2 In five years Edward visited 45 different countries.
3 Edward never got out of his car and talked to people.
4 Edward liked Wallis because she told him the truth.
5 Wallis wanted to talk about central heating.

Read Chapter 5. Put these sentences in the correct order.

1 During the next three years, they became good friends.
2 One night Winfield hit her and locked her in a room.
3 A year later she married Ernest Simpson.
4 A few months later Edward asked Wallis to marry him.
5 Wallis married Winfield Spencer when she was twenty.
6 Two years after that, she met Edward at a house party.
7 There, they fell in love.
8 So Wallis divorced him.
9 Then Edward asked Wallis to go skiing in Austria.

Read Chapters 6 to 8. Who said or wrote this, and to whom?

1 'Be a good King, Edward. And be good to your mother.'
2 'The King is dead. Long live the King.'
3 'I love you more than ever, and you will be my Queen.'
4 'I'll never forget you, but I have to be free.'
5 'I will do what you ask, but I'll never stop loving you.'
6 'Divorce is wrong in the eyes of God!'
7 'I have God on my side, and that is all I need.'
8 'You want to be modern, but the people don't like it.'
9 'We will not have this woman as our Queen.'
10 'You're a King! You must love your country first!'
11 'You're a free man. You must stand and fight.'
12 'My enemies are stronger than I am.'

Before you read Chapters 9 and 10, can you guess what happens? Tick one box for each sentence.

		YES	NO
1	Edward's brother George becomes King.	☐	☐
2	Edward stays in England because the people still want him, not George, as their King.	☐	☐
3	Winston Churchill becomes Prime Minister and tries to help Edward.	☐	☐
4	Edward leaves England and goes to France.	☐	☐
5	Edward marries Wallis in France.	☐	☐
6	All the Royal Family go to the wedding.	☐	☐
7	King George VI dies and Edward becomes King again.	☐	☐
8	Edward and Wallis come back to England and live quietly at Windsor.	☐	☐

Read Chapters 9 to 12, and then answer these questions.

1 What were Edward's and Wallis's new names?
2 Why did Edward return to England in 1952 and in 1961?
3 What happened at a small party in London in 1966?
4 What didn't Wallis like about Edward?
5 Why did Edward give Wallis so many jewels?
6 When did Wallis first enter Buckingham Palace?
7 Where were Edward and Wallis buried?
8 What did Edward think was the most wonderful thing in the world?

ACTIVITIES

After Reading

1 Here are Edward and his brother George arguing, a few days before Edward left England. Put their conversation in the correct order, and write in the speakers' names. George speaks first (number 5).

1 _____ 'He said that you cannot marry Mrs Simpson.'

2 _____ 'Don't call her "this woman" – her name's Wallis. I'm going to marry her, and I'll give the crown to you.'

3 _____ 'Love! You must put your country before love! If you marry her, I never want to see you again.'

4 _____ 'Why can't I? Is it a crime to want to marry?'

5 _____ 'Edward, Mr Baldwin has just been to see me.'

6 _____ 'But you will come to my wedding, won't you?'

7 _____ 'But I don't want it! It's your job to be King, not mine! I've never wanted to be King.'

8 _____ 'And what did he say to you, George?'

9 _____ 'No, I won't. I don't like that woman, and I don't want to see her as your wife.'

10 _____ 'But someone has to be King, George. And it will have to be you because I can't live without Wallis, or without love.'

11 _____ 'Don't be stupid. Of course it's not a crime. But the Church won't have this woman as the Queen.'

2 Find these words in the word search below, and draw a line through them. The words go from left to right, and from top to bottom.

archbishop, bury, crown, disappoint, divorce, dream, jewellery, kiss, newspaper, palace, prime minister, queen, ring, royal, wedding

A	I	W	E	D	D	I	N	G	F	D	Y	O
R	J	E	W	E	L	L	E	R	Y	I	U	N
C	M	A	R	R	R	Y	K	I	S	S	T	E
H	Q	H	O	D	A	T	W	P	O	A	M	W
B	U	R	Y	I	A	N	Y	A	O	P	U	S
I	E	I	A	V	D	W	C	L	I	P	L	P
S	E	N	L	O	R	L	R	A	B	O	R	A
H	N	G	E	R	E	A	O	C	K	I	M	P
O	Y	H	E	C	A	A	W	E	R	N	T	E
P	R	I	M	E	M	I	N	I	S	T	E	R

Now write down all the letters that don't have a line through them, beginning with the first line and going across each line to the end. You will have 38 letters, which will make a sentence of 10 words.

1 What is the sentence?
2 Who said it, and to whom?
3 Who was the speaker talking about?
4 What happened the next day?

3 **Do you agree (A) or disagree (D) with these sentences? Explain why.**

1 Edward was right to marry Wallis. Love is the most important thing in the world.

2 Wallis married Edward because he was rich and famous.

3 The British Royal Family were very unkind to Edward.

4 Photographers should leave royal families alone. They need a private life just like other people.

4 **What kind of person would you like the king (or queen, president, prime minister, etc.) to be? Put this list in order, 1 to 12, beginning with 1 for the most important thing.**

I would like the _____ of my country . . .

- to be clever
- to be kind
- to be a man
- to be a woman
- to be good-looking
- to be well-dressed
- to be a good speaker
- to be a good listener
- to speak many languages
- to be hard-working
- to have a happy family
- to travel by bicycle

5 **Here are some different titles for this story. Which ones do you think are the best? Why? Can *you* think of some titles?**

A Weak King

Edward and Wallis

Long Live Love!

Love Before a Crown

Edward VIII and George VI

A King without a Crown

6 **Read this newspaper article about Edward and Wallis. Can you find and correct the mistakes in it?**

DUKE OF WINDSOR DIES

Edward, Duke of Windsor, died in New York last week. His brother George was by his side during his last hours. The body of the Duke was taken to England by boat, but his wife Wallis did not travel with the Duke's body. The Duke was buried in London.

The love story of Edward and Wallis Simpson shook the world in the 1920s. Edward gave away his crown to his sister Elizabeth because he wanted to marry Mrs Simpson, a divorced Australian woman. They were married for 45 years, and for most of that time they lived in England. They never gave parties, and travelled only to the United States.

The Duchess of Windsor will soon return to her home in Baltimore. She plans to live there with her sister.

7 **Write a paragraph about one of the British Royal Family, or a famous person (a king, queen, president, etc.) from your own country. Use these words to help you.**

- *was born in / mother and father / lived in . . .*
- *When he/she was young/old . . .*
- *loved / married . . . / had . . . children*
- *is famous because . . .*
- *died in / After his/her death . . .*

ABOUT THE AUTHOR

Peter Dainty studied modern history at the University of Oxford. He has worked in English Language Teaching for many years, at a private language school and the University of London, and has taught students from all over the world. He now works as a full-time writer and has published twelve books.

He wrote *The Love of a King* because he thinks that the romance between Edward and Mrs Simpson is a very different and interesting love story. After Edward married Mrs Simpson, he wrote a book, *A King's Story*, which describes his early life in Buckingham Palace when he was a sad and lonely child. He was rich and he was famous, but there was one important thing missing in his life, and that was love. It took him thirty-six years to find love, and when he did, he left his crown, his country, his family, and most of his friends because he wanted to be with Wallis. Some people think he was right to do this, and some people think he was wrong. But nobody can forget the story of a man who was King of forty-two countries, and who gave it all away because he found true love.

ABOUT BOOKWORMS

OXFORD BOOKWORMS LIBRARY
Classics • True Stories • Fantasy & Horror • Human Interest
Crime & Mystery • Thriller & Adventure

The OXFORD BOOKWORMS LIBRARY offers a wide range of original and adapted stories, both classic and modern, which take learners from elementary to advanced level through six carefully graded language stages:

Stage 1 (400 headwords)	**Stage 4** (1400 headwords)
Stage 2 (700 headwords)	**Stage 5** (1800 headwords)
Stage 3 (1000 headwords)	**Stage 6** (2500 headwords)

More than fifty titles are also available on cassette, and there are many titles at Stages 1 to 4 which are specially recommended for younger learners. In addition to the introductions and activities in each Bookworm, resource material includes photocopiable test worksheets and Teacher's Handbooks, which contain advice on running a class library and using cassettes, and the answers for the activities in the books.

Several other series are linked to the OXFORD BOOKWORMS LIBRARY. They range from highly illustrated readers for young learners, to playscripts, non-fiction readers, and unsimplified texts for advanced learners.

Oxford Bookworms Starters	*Oxford Bookworms Factfiles*
Oxford Bookworms Playscripts	*Oxford Bookworms Collection*

Details of these series and a full list of all titles in the OXFORD BOOKWORMS LIBRARY can be found in the *Oxford English* catalogues. A selection of titles from the OXFORD BOOKWORMS LIBRARY can be found on the next pages.

BOOKWORMS · TRUE STORIES · STAGE 2

Henry VIII and his Six Wives

JANET HARDY-GOULD

There were six of them – three Katherines, two Annes, and a Jane. One of them was the King's wife for twenty-four years, another for only a year and a half. One died, two were divorced, and two were beheaded. It was a dangerous, uncertain life.

After the King's death in 1547, his sixth wife finds a box of old letters – one from each of the first five wives. They are sad, angry, frightened letters. They tell the story of what it was like to be the wife of Henry VIII of England.

BOOKWORMS · TRUE STORIES · STAGE 2

William Shakespeare

JENNIFER BASSETT

William Shakespeare. Born April 1564, at Stratford-upon-Avon. Died April 1616. Married Anne Hathaway: two daughters, one son. Actor, poet, famous playwright. Wrote nearly forty plays.

But what was he like as a man? What did he think about when he rode into London for the first time . . . or when he was writing his plays *Hamlet* and *Romeo and Juliet* . . . or when his only son died?

We know the facts of his life, but we can only guess at his hopes, his fears, his dreams.

BOOKWORMS · TRUE STORIES · STAGE 2

Grace Darling

TIM VICARY

All they could hear was the wind, and the waves crashing on to the rocks. All they could see was the night. They could not see the ship, broken in two. They could not see the people holding on to the dark wet rock, slowly dying of cold. And they could not hear the cries for help – only the wind.

How could they save the people on the rock? Was their wooden boat stronger than the iron ship? Were a man and his daughter stronger than the great waves that broke the ship in two?

The *Forfarshire* was wrecked off the north-east coast of England in 1838. This is the true story of Grace Darling – a girl who became a famous heroine on that stormy night.

BOOKWORMS · HUMAN INTEREST · STAGE 2

New Yorkers

O. HENRY

Retold by Diane Mowat

A housewife, a tramp, a lawyer, a waitress, an actress – ordinary people living ordinary lives in New York at the beginning of this century. The city has changed greatly since that time, but its people are much the same. Some are rich, some are poor, some are happy, some are sad, some have found love, some are looking for love.

O. Henry's famous short stories – sensitive, funny, sympathetic – give us vivid pictures of the everyday lives of these New Yorkers.

BOOKWORMS • FANTASY & HORROR • STAGE 2

Return to Earth

JOHN CHRISTOPHER

Retold by Susan Binder

As they walk through a park in the distant future, Harl and Ellen talk about their work and their lives. But they will never have a life together because their work as scientists is more important to them than their love. Harl plans to leave Earth, on a long and dangerous journey through space. Ellen plans to stay on Earth, to change the way the human mind works.

When Harl returns to Earth, Ellen will be long dead . . . and the world will be a very different place.

BOOKWORMS • THRILLER & ADVENTURE • STAGE 3

The Prisoner of Zenda

ANTHONY HOPE

Retold by Diane Mowat

'We must leave for Zenda at once, to find the King!' cried Sapt. 'If we're caught, we'll all be killed!'

So Rudolf Rassendyll and Sapt gallop through the night to find the King of Ruritania. But the King is now a prisoner in the Castle of Zenda. Who will rescue him from his enemies, the dangerous Duke Michael and Rupert of Hentzau?

And who will win the heart of the beautiful Princess Flavia?